Tracks of God

Clair and Retha Shultz

Chinaberry House
P. O. Box 505
Anderson, Indiana 46015-0505
www.2Lights.com

ISBN 10: 1-933858-16-8
ISBN 13: 978-1-933858-16-6
Printed in the United States of America

Acknowledgements

Pat McCune for the many hours of composition and typing.
Dale Stultz for the appropriate, hard-to-find pictures
David Coolidge for editing
Gene W. Newberry for his composition.
Henry Gariepy – excepts from his book "100 Portraits of Christ"
David Liverett – invaluable help with the essentials of preparation
for printing and the use of his drawings and photos
Tammy Burrell – layout
Retha Shultz — many things too numerous to mention.
Poetry by Clair Wilson Shultz
All thanks to our great helper, God, whose tracks are everywhere.

...*"That rainbow is a sign. It is the sign of the agreement that I made with all living things on earth."*

– Genesis 9:17

Table of Contents

All Poems by Clair Wilson Shultz except where indicated.

Introduction

Over the years multitudes have come to believe that God exists and is omnipotent, but the age-old and all-prevailing question is and has always been... "WHERE IS HE?"

God is an all-powerful and divine Spirit, the Creator of the heavens and the earth. And as such, He has the ability to be everywhere on our planet and beyond. He can choose to be seen or remain unseen. The purpose of this book is to show that He only remains "unseen" if we CHOOSE NOT TO SEE. He reveals Himself night and day. All we have to do is sharpen our awareness and look for His "tracks."

Behold...The Tracks of God!

How many times have you heard non-believers say they need to see God to believe in His existence? I intend to explore the myriad ways that God shows us, each and every day, that He is present...and VISIBLE! He leaves His "tracks" in full view...if we just take the time and make the effort, to see them!

Genesis 1:1-2 "In the beginning God created the sky and the earth. The earth was empty and had no form. Darkness covered the ocean, and God's Spirit was moving over the water."

Job 26:7 "God stretches the northern sky out over empty space. And he hangs the earth on nothing."

"...His name will be...Powerful God,..." (Isaiah 9:6)

Although we cannot see God as a physical being, He leaves His "tracks" all around us...indicating His person and His presence.

I would like to start this book by sharing with you the very personal story of my conversion. I can now look back on my long life and see very clearly God's tracks.

God made very special arrangements, which eventually led to my conversion and my lifelong joy of serving Him. Two of my older brothers went along on a trip with a neighbor boy who needed to go to California due to health concerns. In those days, we didn't hop on a plane and arrive at our destination in a few hours. The trip took almost five months in an old Ford car. But when the boys arrived in California they visited some young Christian friends and through their contact with these servants of God they were converted.

After about a year, my brothers returned to our home in Ohio where they shared their experiences with the family. Through their changed lives my parents and the whole family found salvation. I was about six years old at the time.

As I grew and learned to trust God, He began laying a path for me to follow. One of my older brothers traveled to Anderson to go to a Bible college, now Anderson University. When I graduated from high school, this same brother approached me with a proposition. He wanted me to travel to Anderson, Indiana and attend the same college. He said he would pay my expenses until I could get settled and make my own way.

I was thrilled about going to school and was sure God's hand was in the venture. Little did I know that He had even greater things in store for me, for it was there that I met my lifemate and partner for the ministry. I met my wife of seventy years. We were called to the mission field where our combined talents, with God's loving direction, led us on a thirty-three year adventure as world missionaries. We experienced myriad trials and joys over those years and hope to convey to you in this book how blessed we were to have realized God's plan for us at an early age.

I hope that you, too, have realized His presence as it relates to you personally. If not, just open your eyes and your heart and view His *tracks*.

In Psalm 19:1-6 it reads:
"The heavens tell the glory of God. And the skies announce what his hands have made. Day after day they tell the story. Night after night they tell it again. They have no speech or words. They don't make any sound to be heard. But their message goes out through all the world. It goes everywhere on earth. The sky is like a home for the sun. The sun comes out like a bridegroom from his bedroom. It rejoices like an athlete eager to run a race. The sun rises at one end of the sky, and it follows its path to the other end. Nothing hides from its heat."

Don't just look...listen...and feel...and smell. Use your God-given senses to reveal God's *tracks*. What do you have to lose? And you have so much to gain.

The Tracks of God

racks left behind, in the mud or the snow
Reveal certain things we always can know.
Tracks identify an animal, like a fox or a cow,
Without viewing its body...tracks reveal how!

Objects leave tracks that do not lie.
Like the vapor trail of a plane, high up in the sky.
Criminals leave tracks, like the print of fingers,
And a skunk is perceived through his smell that lingers!

Well, God's tracks can be seen, in the growing embryo of a child...
Only two cells to begin...then growth goes wild!
Imagine! Developing its own anatomy, with brain, lungs and heart...
And millions of cellular connections...without missing a part!

God's tracks are to be noted in the winds that blow,
Bringing oceans of rain that make crops grow.
His might is seen in our two eyes that see...
And in multiple fruits, pollinated by His bee.

We cannot see God in a bodily way,
But we can see His tracks by night and by day.
In earth's orbiting of the sun with its heat and its light,
Sole sustainer in our world of every form of life.

"I Spy" Tracks

A family with young children was once taking an automobile trip. On the way the children became somewhat rowdy, as is common for young children to do when they become a bit bored. So they decided to play a game called "Tracks." The object of the game was to scour their surroundings as they motored through the countryside and identify any objects or occurrences they "spied" which revealed the evidence of God's presence...or His "tracks." Whenever they spied a "track" of God, they were to shout out, "I spy," and then they would point out the "tracks" they saw.

We can all play that game every day and become more aware of His presence. Interestingly enough, we can all look at the same spot and see different tracks. One person can look out a window and see mud and rocks, while another can look out the same window and see the wind blowing the tree branches, a chickadee pecking at a berry, a furry little striped chipmunk joyfully dancing across the green grass, or a lady bug sauntering up a daffodil stem. Our world, created by God, is not a boring place. We just have to take the time to recognize the bundles of joy that God has laid before us!

Try this game with your children, grandchildren, or friends. It allows wonderful insight into different individual's perceptions of God.

The Wondrous Plans of God

I do not know how an apple tree can make an apple red,
I just rejoice that trees make food, and I am fed.

I do not know how the humming bird sips nectar on the wing.
I only know that as it flies, its mission is God's thing.

I do not know how a nut is formed high up in a walnut tree,
I only know that here and there, a squirrel is quick to see.

I do not know how a carrot grows or flowers turn toward light.
But this I know that the clouds bring rain and the sun is warm and bright.

I do not know how God builds worlds, that stand, and last forever,
But this I know, God's plans are good – will never fail us – never!

It Exists

A track of God is a power that does not have to be seen to exist.

Electricity is not visible as it zips along the wire from Anderson to Port of Spain, Trinidad and all places. But, as it runs, it is doing many things: such as turning a motor a thousand miles away, unseen. At Kima in Kenya where we lived we had heavy power lines running through the compound.

We also had fruit bats that landed on the wire upside down. But the power company added a ground wire. The bats knew that they had landed on the wires before and it was all right, but when they came searching for food, landed on the top wire, and their bodies fell downward to the bottom wire and touched two wires they were killed. They did not understand electricity.

Although God cannot be seen in a physical form, there are marks or tracks of His being which clearly indicate His person and presence. This reasoning can be illustrated by several examples.

Certain kinds of tracks left behind in the snow give identification to the animal which made them. Example – rabbit. Although an animal is not present, it leaves signs of its existence. For example, animal tracks left in the snow are usually distinctive and identifiable. A rabbit's tracks differ from a cat's tracks. And all tracks are evidence that something has been in that location…even though we can no longer see it, it was there. It exists.

A certain distinct sound clearly identifies its source. Example – a wild turkey. Sounds may be indicative of something's existence. An animal's painful cry or soulful mating call indicates its presence though it isn't necessarily visible. And we don't question its presence. If we hear a bear growl, chances are we won't ponder its existence. We will trust that it is present, and take action.

If the sky is dark and the clouds are churning, and we hear a roaring train, where no train tracks exist...do we trust our senses and believe a tornado or strong winds are present? Or do we discount the storms existence because we cannot see the funnel?

It is not uncommon to see a flock of vultures soaring around and around over a single spot. We see nothing to entice their presence, but common sense and experience tell us a dead animal is nearby. Because we see it? No. But the invisible tracks, indicated by the presence of the vultures, tells us the unseen creature is near.

Have you ever seen the vapor trail in the sky? Certainly. Can we see what left the trail? Sometimes. But our experience tells us a large plane has traveled through the skies, whether it was seen or unseen by us.

Certain things cannot possibly bring about their own existence. Example: a 747 jumbo jet plane as it flies through the air at 600 miles per hour, while carrying 400 passengers, non-stop with all their luggage from London to New York. Do you think that it just happens to exist by itself? The guidance system itself is a modern miracle. One may not know who built it or where it was built or how it was done, but one would have to conclude that smart brains of many people with specialized equipment would be necessary to make such a plane.

A certain sound of a loud roar in East Africa indicates the nearby presence of a lion. A friend of ours from the United States wanted to see a lion. He had to find a toilet several times in the night. He found one just outside the house. The way even was lighted. In the morning he happened to look and not more than five feet away, near the wheels of the car, were three large lion tracks, the size of which measured close to 10 inches. The next night he found something inside to use. "Tracks" were enough.

The presence of a skunk is indicated by the smell that lingers.

The presence of a mosquito can be recognized by the malaria it carries.

Tiny wood pellets in a little pile on the floor under the woodwork, or in the piano, indicate the existence of termites. When we saw these, we would fill a hypodermic needle with insecticide to insert in the hole from which the pellets were coming to kill the insects that were eating the wood.

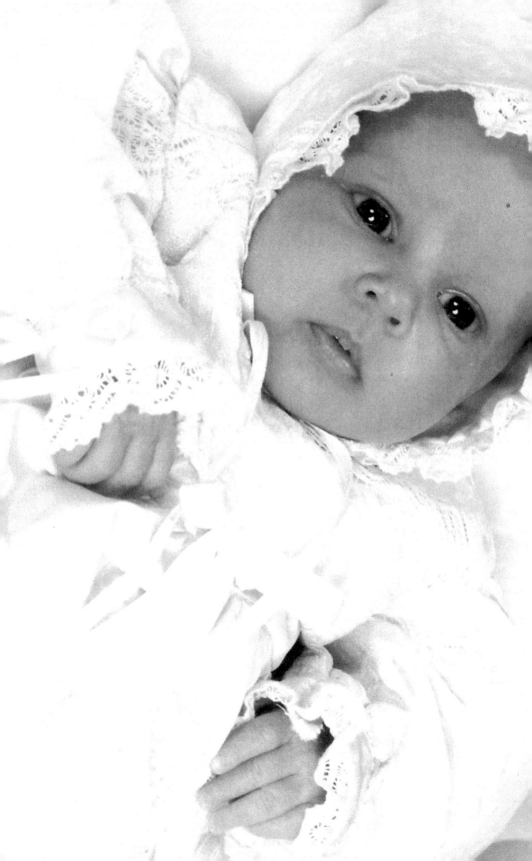

Life Begins

The supernatural tracks of God are revealed in all forms of life, whether it be in a nut or an egg or a horse or a human being or a tree. When God had created man he discovered man needed someone to help him do the things the man was not created to do. So he created woman – somewhat like a man – but it took the two of them to make one whole person – not two men, not two women. The race was to be increased by the union of two beings – a complete whole being – man and woman, to make a new creature, a baby, who would be born of love between two beings who have become one, to be loved as only a whole person – man and woman – are equipped to do.

Think of the magnitude of the way a tiny egg and sperm can be united to develop in a small cavity of the mother. The cells unite in a certain pattern by themselves, with no light or direction in a nine-month period, developing into the entirety of a human life with millions of microscopic cells, making themselves into different organs and parts of the body: a nose with nostrils, eyes with color and vision, five fingers on each hand, two arms, eyebrows, eyelashes, two ears that hear the tiniest of sounds, two kidneys, ten toes, taste buds that transform eating from a necessity for life into a joy, a skull covering a brain that directs all the rest of the body, a heart that pumps blood through thousands of feet of veins and arteries, a liver, a stomach, lungs, procreation organs, hair, teeth at the proper time, important glands... And if creating all these entities was not in and of itself a miracle...all parts must function together in perfect harmony to produce one normal human being.

The most skilled surgeon with the most modern equipment cannot produce one single human organ in the lab. But we can see evidence of someone or something that had to be perfect to produce a child with all its parts in all the right places. Feet with toenails, joints, sex organs, ears, its feet in the right place, its mouth and teeth and head, lungs breathing in perfect sequence, to create a new life...everything placed where it functions and does its assigned work. Where it belongs so the whole baby can live as a unit with everything going as is necessary for living and reproduction of itself into a new perfect body. Small glands that make everything work in the whole body is almost unthinkable. What if the eye were placed in the foot position? What if the nose were placed where the feet must carry on? How does the eye know how the eyelid is to work in perfect order? Think of it, when the baby is born, every part is in its own place, even the eyelid, keeping the eye clean in dusty situations. Fluids jet in place to keep the eyeball clean. Everything is absolutely in place and operating for the hearing. Digestion without teeth for about a year and then the teeth come into the mouth as needed.

The human brain weighs three to four pounds but contains about 100 billion neurons (nerve cells). Although that extraordinary number is of the same order of magnitude as the number of stars in the Milky Way, it cannot account for the complexity of the brain. –Gerald D. Fischback, M.D. "Mind and Brain"

How is memory stored in the brain cells? I remember events that happened ninety years ago about my family. Where and how was this memory retained for ninety years without being lost?

As an example – During World War One, my mother would hold me on her lap and read news about the war. When it was over I was so elated, I wanted the whole world to know. So I made a sign and nailed it to a post so all could see, "WE WON THE WAR."

The agnostic might argue that it is the nature of the body to make itself. That is true. But where did this "nature" come from? For example, it is the nature of a washing machine to wash clothes. True. But there has to be someone who designed the first one and got a patent on the design. Who holds the patent on the body design? In the beginning, someone had to design these various cells working in cooperation and in sequence to make the body operational.

Bone

Much life consists of flesh and bone. Consider how life continues. It begins through the sex organs of all animals – male and female. We will consider only humans. The man provides what is called sperm and the woman provides an egg. The two are brought together through the wonderful experience of sex. The male will give a small part of himself and the woman will give a small part of herself and they will get together. I have previously told about the development of the brain, but not about bone. This is all good and wonderful, but it wouldn't do any good without bone. Without the bone the body could not operate. What is it between flesh and bone? A great difference. They all have their beginning in the same place, but they are all different. What could an arm or leg do without a bone, or bone around the brain to hold it? So all creatures in some ways are alike. They must have flesh and bone – a lion, an elephant, a dog, a human being. It's what enables the flesh to operate and fulfill its purpose. The brain is the most wonderful creation. I have previously described it as a track of God, but without a bone it would be useless. The same two cells between a man and a woman were working together producing a man or woman, wonderful flesh, wonderful BONE! – The Track of God!

Rainbows

Genesis 9:8-17

 hen God said to Noah and his sons, "Now I am making my agreement with you and your people who will live after you. And I also make it with every living thing that is with you. It is with the birds, the tame animals and the wild animals. It is with all that came out of the boat with you. I make my agreement with every living thing on earth. I make this agreement with you: I will never again destroy all living things by floodwaters. A flood will never again destroy the earth."

And God said, "I am making an agreement between me and you and every living creature that is with you. It will continue from now on. This is the sign: I am putting my rainbow in the clouds. It is the sign of the agreement between me and the earth. When I bring clouds over the earth, a rainbow appears in the clouds. Then I will remember my agreement between me and you and every living thing. Floodwaters will never again destroy all life on the earth. When the rainbow appears in the clouds, I will see it. Then I will remember the agreement that continues forever between me and every living thing on the earth."

So God said to Noah, "That rainbow is a sign. It is the sign of the agreement that I made with all living things on earth."

The Solar System
Genesis 15:5

onsider the magnitude of unthinkable genius manifested in our solar system. Our large earth is 8000 thousand miles in diameter, twenty-five thousand miles in circumference and is suspended in space with an invisible magnetic attachment to the sun, ninety-three million miles distance. If the sun were closer to the earth, the earth would burn up; if farther away it would be too cold for life to exist. Everything depends on the sun for its existence. The sun gives light, heat, growth of trees, vegetation, oxygen, lifts up water to purify it. The earth is moving in a giant orbit around the sun at a fast speed that holds the earth the same distance from the sun. One orbit takes 365 days to complete. Too, our earth makes one complete revolution in twenty-four hours so that, as it turns facing the sun, each part will receive adequate warmth and light.

One more thing: the axes of our earth are not set perpendicular to the face of the sun, but rather are set at a twenty-two degree angle to the sun's face. If this were not this way, then that part of the earth at its poles would never have enough light or heat. When the earth is half way around the sun in this tilted position, one pole is more exposed to the heat. The other pole then has its share of light and heat. How amazing and wonderful.

The tracks of God are everywhere. It is much easier to believe in God as the Great Creator who alone had the intelligence and ability to create life as we know it on the earth and the genius that created our solar system than not to believe it.

There is no intelligent explanation without God. Psalm 19, written by King David, a thousand years before Rome ruled, wrote this psalm after looking at the firmament in his day. In Psalm 19:1-6, he wrote: "The heavens tell the glory of God. And the skies announce what his hands have made. Day after day they tell the story. Night after night they tell it again. They have no speech or words. They don't make any sound to be heard. But their message goes out through all the world. It goes everywhere on earth. The sky is like a home for the sun. The sun comes out like a bridegroom from his bedroom. It rejoices like an athlete eager to run a race. The sun rises at one end of the sky, and it follows its path to the other end. Nothing hides from its heat."

Wonderful! Wonderful! Wonderful!

Meteor Track

Biblical Tracks

God's tracks were evident in the ways He protected His leaders in the Old Testament.

Joseph

Joseph was born to Jacob and was a favorite son. His father made him a coat of many colors.

One time Joseph was sent to look for his brothers to see if they were all right. They saw him coming and because Joseph had a dream he told his brothers about, they hated him. "Listen to the dream I had. We were in the field tying bundles of wheat. My bundle stood up and your bundles bowed down to mine." His brothers said, "Do you really think you will be king over us?" His brothers hated him even more. Joseph's brothers saw him coming from far away. Before he reached them, they made a plan to kill him. They said to each other, "Here comes that dreamer. Let's kill him and throw his body into one of the wells. We can tell our father that a wild animal killed him. Then we will see what will become of his dreams." So when Joseph came to his brothers, they pulled off his robe with long sleeves. Then they threw him into the well. It was empty. There was no water in it. While Joseph was in the well, the brothers sat down to eat. While they were deciding what to do with him, some Egyptians came along. They decided to sell him to the Egyptians instead of putting him in a well. So Joseph was taken to Egypt where he was put in prison. Through many hard times in prison, he was brought to Pharaoh for whom he interpreted a dream. In the dream there would be seven good years and seven bad years. Joseph recommended to Pharaoh that he appoint a ruler who would plant many crops during the good years to be used in the bad years. Pharaoh thought this was a good plan, so he appointed Joseph as ruler of Egypt. Joseph had the Egyptians raise much food for seven good years. Then the bad years came and Joseph's family needed food, so they came to Egypt to get food. God had preserved Joseph through many problems in order to give his family food in the bad times.

God's tracks are seen through the many ways he preserved his leaders.

Moses

Exodus 1: 8-10 & 22
Exodus 2: 1-21; 3:1-5 & 7-10

Exodus 1:8-10 Then a new king began to rule Egypt. He did not know who Joseph was. This king said to his people, "Look! The people of Israel are too many! And they are too strong for us to handle! We must make plans against them. If we don't, the number of their people will grow even more. Then if there is a war, they might join our enemies. Then they could fight us and escape from the country!"

Exodus 1:22 So the king commanded all his people: "Every time a boy is born to the Hebrews, you must throw him into the Nile River, but let all the girl babies live."

Exodus 2:1-21 There was a man from the family of Levi. He married a woman who was also from the family of Levi. She became pregnant and gave birth to a son. She saw how wonderful the baby was, and she hid him for three months. But after three months, she was not able to hide the baby any longer. So she got a basket and covered it with tar so that it would float. She put the baby in the basket. Then she put the basket among the tall grass at the edge of the Nile River. The baby's sister stood a short distance away. She wanted to see what would happen to him.

Then the daughter of the king of Egypt came to the river. She was going to take a bath. Her servant girls were walking beside the river. She saw the basket in the tall grass. So she sent her slave girl to get it.

The king's daughter opened the basket and saw the baby boy. He was crying and she felt sorry for him. She said "This is one of the Hebrew babies."

Then the baby's sister asked the king's daughter, "Would you like me to find a Hebrew woman to nurse the baby for you?"

The king's daughter said, "Yes please." So the girl went and got the baby's own mother.

The king's daughter said to the woman, "Take this baby and nurse him for me. I will pay you." So the woman took her baby and nursed him. After the child had grown older, the woman took him to the king's daughter. She adopted the baby as her own son. The king's daughter named him Moses, because she had pulled him out of the water.

(How God's tracks can be seen. He arranged for Moses' own mother to nurse him – with pay – and he grew and became a man.)

Moses grew and became a man. One day he visited his people, the Hebrews. He saw that they were forced to work very hard. He saw an Egyptian beating a Hebrew man, one of Moses' own people. Moses looked all around and saw that no one was watching. So he killed the Egyptian and hid his body in the sand.

The next day Moses returned and saw two Hebrew men fighting each other. He saw that one man was in the wrong. Moses said to that man, "Why are you hitting one of your own people?"

The man answered, "Who made you our ruler and judge? Are you going to kill me as you killed the Egyptian?"

Then Moses was afraid. He thought, "Now everyone knows what I did."

When the king heard about what Moses had done, he tried to kill

Moses. But Moses ran away from the king and went to live in the land of Midian. There he sat down near a well.

There was a priest in Midian who had seven daughters. His daughters went to that well to get water for their father's sheep. They were trying to fill the water troughs for their father's sheep. But some shepherds came and chased the girls away. Then Moses defended the girls and watered their sheep.

Then they went back to their father, Reuel, also called Jethro. He asked them, "Why have you come home early today?"

The girls answered, "The shepherds chased us away. But an Egyptian defended us. He got water for us and watered our sheep."

He asked his daughters, "Where is this man? Why did you leave him? Invite him to eat with us."

Moses stayed with Jethro. And he gave his daughter Zipporah to Moses to be his wife.

Exodus 2:23-24 After a long time, the king of Egypt died. The people of Israel groaned because they were made to work very hard. They cried for help. And God heard them. God heard their cries, and he remembered the agreement he had made with Abraham, Isaac and Jacob.

Exodus 3:1-5 One day Moses was taking care of Jethro's sheep. Jethro was the priest of Midian and also Moses' father-in-law. Moses led the sheep to the west side of the desert. He came to Sinai, the mountain of God. There the angel of the Lord appeared to Moses in the flames of fire coming out of a bush. Moses saw that the bush was on fire, but it was not burning up. So Moses said, "I will go closer to this strange thing. How can a bush continue burning without burning up?"

The Lord saw Moses was coming to look at the bush. So God called to him from the bush, "Moses, Moses!"

And Moses said, "here I am."

Then God said, "Do not come any closer. Take off your sandals. You are standing on holy ground."

Exodus 3:7-10 The Lord said, "I have seen the troubles my people have suffered in Egypt. And I have heard their cries when the Egyptian slave masters hurt them. I am concerned about their pain. I have come down to save them from the Egyptians. I will bring them out of that land...I am sending you to the king of Egypt. Go! Bring my people, the Israelites. out of Egypt!"

So God had preserved Moses as a baby in order that he might lead the Israelites out of Egypt.

Ruth

od's track in the ancestry of Jesus showing He was both Jew and Gentile. Jesus was a world person.

One of the most interesting parts of this story of Ruth is the manner in which Jesus became a part of the human race of all people of the world, NOT JUST JEWISH people. Thus, His human ancestors were a mixture of Jew and Gentile not just Jew. (See story in Ruth 1:1-22. Read the whole story in book of Ruth).

Because of the way Boaz treated Ruth she said, "you have given me hope."

Because Ruth became an ancestor of Jesus, everyone can have hope. This is why the church has sent missionaries to all the world.

Ruth was a Gentile woman, married to Naomi's son Mahlon, a Jewish man. Naomi's husband, Elimelech, died and Ruth's husband, Mahlon, who was Naomi's son, died. Ruth decided to stay with her mother-in-law, even though Naomi urged her to return to her people. As was the custom, if a husband dies, a sibling or close family member is to marry and care for the widowed woman. In the course of time, Naomi instructed Ruth to go to Boaz, a close relative of Naomi's family.

Through Naomi's planning, Boaz purchased back the land of Elimelech, husband of Naomi, to keep the land in the family. As was the custom at the time, he also took Ruth as his wife, thus joining the Jewish and Gentiles in marriage. Boaz said, "She is the Moabite who is the wife of Mahlon. I am doing this so her dead husband's portion will stay with his family. This way his name will not be separated from his family and his land." And that union produced Jesse, the father of David. So the tracks of God are evident in arranging a union which was not exclusively Jewish, which would eventually lead to the birth of Jesus!

And because Ruth had a son, Naomi had a grandson. Naomi took the boy, held him in her arms and cared for him. In the same way, may the Lord give you many children through Ruth and may your family be great through him. So Naomi took the boy, held him in her arms and cared for him. The boy was born for Naomi and the neighbors named him Obed because he was born for Naomi. Obed was Jesse's father and Jesse was the father of David and David was the ancestor of Jesus.

So through the heartache which occurred with the tragic losses of Naomi's husband and sons, we can see God's plan...his tracks...which led to the eventual birth of Jesus. And in His infinite wisdom, God arranged a union which was not a Jewish union, but a combination of Jewish and Gentile backgrounds.

David

I Samuel 17: 4-10, 16--17, 19-23, 26, 31-51

The Philistines had a champion fighter named Goliath. He was from Gath. He was about nine feet four inches tall. He came out of the Philistine camp. He had a bronze helmet on his head. And he wore a coat of scale armor. It was made of bronze and weighed about 125 pounds. He wore bronze protectors on his legs. And he had a small spear of bronze tied on his back. The wooden part of his larger spear was like a weaver's rod. And its blade weighed about fifteen pounds. The officer who carried his shield walked in front of him.

Goliath stood and shouted to the Israelite soldiers, "Why have you taken positions for battle? I am a Philistine, and you are Saul's servants! Choose a man and send him to fight me. If he can fight and kill me, we will become your servants. But if I defeat and kill him, you will become our servants." Then he said, "Today I stand and dare the army of Israel! Send one of your men to fight me!"

The Philistine came out every morning and evening. He stood before the Israelite army. This continued for forty days.

Now David was the son of Jesse, an Ethrathite. Jesse was from Bethlehem in Judah. He had eight sons. David was the youngest son. David went back and forth from Saul to Bethlehem. There he took care of his father's sheep.

Now Jesse said to his son, David, "Take this half bushel of cooked grain. And take ten loaves of bread. Take them to your brothers in camp....Your brothers are with Saul and the army in the valley of Elah. They are fighting against the Philistines."

Early in the morning David left the sheep with another shepherd. He took the food and left as Jesse had told him. When David arrived at the camp, the army was leaving. They were going out to their battle positions. The soldiers were shouting their war cry. The Israelites and Philistines were lining up their men to face each other in battle.

David left the food with the man who kept the supplies. Then he ran to the battle line and talked with his brothers. While he was talking with them, Goliath came out. He was the Philistine champion from Gath. He shouted things against Israel as usual, and David heard it.

David asked the men who stood near him, "What will be done to reward the man who kills this Philistine? What will be done for whoever takes away the shame from Israel? Goliath is a Philistine. He is not circumcised. Why does he think he can speak against the armies of the living God?"

Some men heard what David said and told Saul. Then Saul ordered David be sent to him.

David said to Saul, "Don't let anyone be discouraged. I, your servant, will go and fight this Philistine!"

Saul answered, "You can't go out against this Philistine and fight him. You're only a boy. Goliath has been a warrior since he was a young man."

But David said to Saul, "I, your servant, have been keeping my father's sheep. When a lion or bear took a sheep from the flock, I would chase it. I would attack it and save the sheep from its mouth. When it attacked me, I caught it by its fur. I would hit it and kill it. I, your servant, have killed both a lion and a bear. Goliath, the Philistine who is not circumcised, will be like the lion or bear I have killed. He will die because he has stood against the armies of the

Living God. The Lord saved me from a lion and a bear. He will also save me from this Philistine.

Saul said to David, "Go, and may the Lord be with you." Saul put his own clothes on David. He put a bronze helmet on David's head and armor on his body. David put on Saul's sword and tried to walk around, but he was not used to all the armor Saul had put on him.

He said to Saul, "I can't go in this. I'm not used to it." Then David took it all off. He took his stick in his hand. And he chose five smooth stones from a stream. He put them in his pouch and held his sling in his hand. Then he went to meet Goliath.

At the same time, the Philistine was coming closer to David. The man who held his shield walked in front of him. Goliath looked at David. He saw that David was only a boy, tanned and handsome. He looked down at David with disgust. He said, "Do you think I am a dog, that you come at me with a stick?" He used his god's name to curse David. He said to David, "Come here. I'll feed your body to the birds of the air and the wild animals."

But David said to him, "You come to me using a sword, a large spear, and a small spear. But I come to you in the name of the Lord of heaven's armies. He's the God of the armies of Israel! You have spoken out against him. Today the Lord will give you to me. I'll kill you, and I'll cut off your head. Today I'll feed the bodies of the Philistine soldiers to the birds of the air and the wild animals. Then all the world will know there is a God in Israel! Everyone gathered here will know the Lord does not need swords or spears to save people. The battle belongs to him! And he will help us defeat all of you."

As Goliath came near to attack him, David ran quickly to meet him. He took a stone from his pouch. He put it into his sling and swung it. The stone hit the Philistine on his forehead and sank into it. Goliath fell facedown on the ground.

So David defeated the Philistine with only a sling and a stone! He hit him and killed him. He did not even have a sword in his hand. David ran and stood beside the Philistine. He took Goliath's sword out of its holder and killed him. Then he cut off Goliath's head. *THE TRACKS OF GOD!!!*

New Testament Tracks

God's Tracks at Jesus' Tomb

Matt. 27:45-46; 50-54, 57-60, 62-66; 28:1-7

When Jesus hung on the cross, at noon the whole country became dark. This darkness lasted for three hours. About three o'clock Jesus cried out in a loud voice, "Eli, Eli, lema sabachthani?" This means, "My God, my God, why have you left me alone?" …Again Jesus cried out in a loud voice. Then Jesus died.

Then the curtain in the Temple split into two pieces. The tear started at the top and tore all the way down to the bottom. Also, the earth shook and rocks broke apart. The graves opened, and many of God's people who had died were raised from death…. They went into the holy city, and many people saw them.

The army officer and the soldiers guarding Jesus saw this earthquake and everything else that happened. They were very frightened and said, "He really was the Son of God!"

That evening a rich man named Joseph came to Jerusalem. He was a follower of Jesus from the town of Arimathea. Joseph went to Pilate and asked to have Jesus' body. Pilate gave orders for the soldiers to give it to Joseph. Then Joseph took the body and

Jesus

wrapped it in a clean linen cloth. He put Jesus' body in a new tomb that he had cut into a wall of rock. He rolled a very large stone to block the entrance of the tomb. Then he went away....

...The next day, the leading priests and the Pharisees went to Pilate. They said, "Sir, we remember that while that liar was still alive he said, 'After three days I will rise from death.' So give the order for the tomb to be guarded closely till the third day. His followers might come and steal the body. Then they could tell the people that he has risen from death. That would be even worse than the first one."

Pilate said, "Take some soldiers and go guard the tomb the best way you know." So they all went to the tomb and made it safe from thieves. They did this by sealing the stone in the entrance and then putting soldiers there to guard it.

The day after the Sabbath day was the first day of the week. At dawn on the first day, Mary Magdalene and another Mary went to look at the tomb.

At that time there was a strong earthquake. An angel of the Lord came down from heaven. The angel went to the tomb and rolled the stone away from the entrance. Then he sat on the stone. He was shining as bright as lightning. His clothes were white as snow. The soldiers guarding the tomb were very frightened of the angel. They shook with fear and then became like dead men.

The angel said to the women, "Don't be afraid. I know you are looking for Jesus, the one who was killed on the cross. But He is not here. He has risen from death as He said He would. Come and see the place where His body was. And go quickly and tell His followers. Say to them: 'Jesus has risen from the death. He is going into Galilee ahead of you. You will see Him there."

(The women were afraid of how the stone would get moved from in front of the tomb but God sent an earthquake and angels to take it away.)

God used tracks of earthquakes and angels!

Fishermen

The disciples had locked themselves in a room for about a week for fear of the Jews, who knew they were followers of Jesus whom the Jews had killed. Simon Peter said, "I am going fishing." Seven other disciples were with Peter. They said to him, "We will go with you." They went out and got into the boat but that night they caught nothing.

Just as the day was breaking Jesus stood on the beach; yet the disciples did not know that it was Jesus. Jesus said to them, "Children, have you any fish?" "No." He said to them, "Cast the net on the right side of the boat and you will find some." So they cast it, and now they were not able to haul it in, for the quantity of fish. That disciple whom Jesus loved said to Peter, "It is the Lord!" When Simon Peter heard that it was the Lord, he put on his clothes, for he was stripped for work, and sprang into the sea. But the other disciples came in the boat, dragging the net full of fish, for they were not far from land, but about a hundred yards off.

When they got out on land, they saw a charcoal fire there, with fish lying on it, and bread. Jesus said to them, "bring some of the fish you have just caught." So Simon Peter went aboard and hauled the net ashore, full of large fish, a hundred and fifty-three of them: although there were so many, the net was not torn. Jesus said to them, "Come and have breakfast." They must have been keenly aware of God's tracks at that particular moment.

The experienced fishermen couldn't catch fish BUT Jesus knew exactly where the fish were. And so it is with us. When we cannot figure out what to do, Jesus knows and comes to our rescue. He comes to us!

Peter

Peter

Acts 12:1-17

uring that same time King Herod began to do terrible things to some who belonged to the church. He ordered James, the brother of John, to be killed by the sword. Herod saw that the Jews liked this, so he decided to arrest Peter, too. (This happened during the time of the Feast of Unleavened Bread.)

After Herod arrested Peter, he put him in jail and handed him over to be guarded by 16 soldiers. Herod planned to bring Peter before the people for trial after the Passover Feast. So Peter was kept in jail. But the church kept on praying to God for him.

The night before Herod was to bring him to trial, Peter was sleeping. He was between two soldiers, bound with two chains. Other soldiers were guarding the door of the jail. Suddenly, an angel of the Lord stood there. A light shined in the room. The angel touched Peter on the side and woke him up. The angel said, "Hurry! Get up!" And the chains fell off Peter's hands. The angel said to him, "Get dressed and put on your sandals," And so Peter did this. Then an angel said, "Put on your coat and follow me." So the angel went out, and Peter followed him. Peter did not know if what the angel was doing was real. He thought he might be seeing a vision. They went past the first and the second guard. They came to the iron gate that separated them from the city. The gate opened itself for them. They went through the gate and walked down a street. And the angel suddenly left him.

Then Peter realized what had happened. He thought, "Now I know that the Lord really sent his angel to me. He rescued me from Herod and from all the things the Jewish people thought would happen."

When he realized this, he went to the home of Mary. She was the mother of John. (John was also called Mark.) Many people were gathered there, praying. Peter knocked on the outside door. A servant girl named Rhonda came to answer it. When she recognized Peter's voice, she was so happy she forgot to open the door. She ran inside and told the group, "Peter is at the door!"

They said to her, "You are crazy!" but she kept on saying that it was true. So they said, "It must be Peter's angel."

Peter continued to knock. When they opened the door, they saw him and were amazed. Peter made a sign with his hand to tell them to be quiet. He explained how the Lord led him out of the jail. And he said, "Tell James and the other believers what happened." Then he left to go to another place.

Acts 9:32-42

As Peter was traveling through all the area, he visited God's people who lived in Lydda. There he met a paralyzed man named Aeneas. Aeneas had not been able to leave his bed for the past eight years. Peter said to him, "Aeneas, Jesus Christ heals you. Stand up and make your bed!" Aeneas stood immediately. All the people living in Lydda and on the Plain of Sharon saw him. These people turned to the Lord. *A Track of God.*

In the city of Joppa there was a follower named Tabitha. (Her Greek name, Dorcas, means "a deer.") She was always doing good and helping the poor. While Peter was in Lydda, Tabitha became sick and died. Her body was washed and put in a room upstairs. The followers in Joppa heard that Peter was in Lydda. (Lydda is near Joppa.) So they sent two men to Peter. They begged him,

"Hurry, please come to us!" Peter got ready and went with them. When he arrived, they took him to the upstairs room. All the widows stood around Peter, crying. They showed him the shirts and coats that Tabitha had made when she was still alive. Peter sent everyone out of the room. He kneeled and prayed. The he turned to the body and said, "Tabitha, stand up!" She opened her eyes, and when she saw Peter, she sat up. He gave her his hand and helped her up. The he called the saints and the widows into the room. He showed them Tabitha; she was alive! People everywhere in Joppa learned about this, and many believed in the Lord. Peter stayed in Joppa for many days with a man named Simon who was a leather-worker. *A Track of God.*

Luke

uke was a Greek physician who did great research about the stories of Jesus.

Luke 1:1-4 To Theophilus: Many have tried to give a history of the things that happened among us. They have written the same things that we learned from others – the people who saw those things from the beginning and served God by telling people his message. I myself studied everything carefully from the beginning, your Excellency. I thought I should write it out for you. So I put it in order in a book. I write these things so that you can know that what you have been taught is true."

Part of Luke's research was done while he was able to stay with Paul in prison and Luke was able to help Paul with his physical needs. *Tracks of God.*

Paul

Acts 9:1-22

In Jerusalem Saul was still trying to frighten the followers of the Lord by saying he would kill them. So he went to the high priest and asked him to write letters to the synagogues in the city of Damascus. Saul wanted the high priest to give him the authority to find people in Damascus who were followers of Christ's Way. If he found any there, men or women, he would arrest them and bring them back to Jerusalem.

So Saul went to Damascus. As he came near the city, a bright light from heaven suddenly flashed around him. Saul fell to the ground. He heard a voice saying to him, "Saul, Saul! Why are you doing things against me?"

Saul said, "Who are you, Lord?"

The voice answered, "I am Jesus. I am the One you are trying to hurt. Get up now and go into the city. Someone there will tell you what you must do."

The men traveling with Saul stood there, but they said nothing. They heard the voice, but they saw no one. Saul got up from the ground. He opened his eyes, but he could not see. So the men with Saul took his hand and led him into Damascus. For three days Saul could not see, and he did not eat or drink.

There was a follower of Jesus in Damascus named Ananias. The Lord spoke to Ananias in a vision, "Ananias!"

Ananias answered, "Here I am, Lord."

Luke

The Lord said to him, "Get up and go to the street called Straight Street. Find the house of Judas. Ask for a man named Saul from the city of Tarsus. He is there now, praying. Saul has seen a vision. In it a man named Ananias comes to him and lays his hands on him. Then he sees again."

But Ananias answered, "Lord, many people have told me about this man and the terrible things he did to your people in Jerusalem. Now he has come here to Damascus. The leading priests have given him the power to arrest everyone who worships you."

But the Lord said to Ananias, "Go! I have chosen Saul for an important work. He must tell about me to non-jews, to kings, and to the people of Israel. I will show him how much he must suffer for my name."

So Ananias went to the house of Judas. He laid his hands on Saul and said, "Brother Saul, the Lord Jesus sent me. He is the one you saw on the road on your way here. He sent me so that you can see again and be filled with the Holy Spirit." Immediately, something that looked like fish scales fell from Saul's eyes. He was able to see again! Then Saul got up and was baptized. After eating some food, his strength returned.

Saul stayed with the followers of Jesus in Damascus for a few days. Soon he began to preach about Jesus in the synagogues, saying, "Jesus is the Son of God!"

All the people who heard him were amazed. They said, "This is the man who was in Jerusalem. He was trying to destroy those who trust in this name! He came here to do the same thing. He came here to arrest the followers of Jesus and take them back to the leading priests."

But Saul became more and more powerful. His proofs that Jesus is the Christ were so strong that the Jews in Damascus could not argue with him. *The Tracks of God.*

*The Tracks of God! We never know what will happen
when each of us seeks God's plan for our living.*

As related by Retha Shultz

Modern Day Tracks

Unprepared

hen we have a job to do and sometimes feel unprepared and inadequate, God can provide whatever we need to triumph over the situation...yet another visible track.

A few years ago I was to be the speaker at the WCG Convention in Fairbanks, Alaska. I was partially ready to speak, but was not satisfied about one of the sections of my speech. Before retiring for the night, I asked God to help me with my talk...to speak through me. At four o'clock in the morning, the day of my speaking engagement, (not a time I would expect to do my best thinking!) I woke up and the thoughts began coming thick and fast. I got my pencil and paper and began taking dictation from my heavenly Father! He provided me with point after point. The response to my talk was overwhelming. It proved to me that God knew what He wanted me to say...all I had to do was ask...and listen!

Loss of a Child

When our daughter Carol was about two years old, we were anticipating the arrival of a baby brother or sister for her. Everything went very well...up to the time of the baby's birth. Shortly before the baby was due, I went for a check up, still believing all was well. However, when labor started and I got to the hospital, the doctor examined me. The doctor said to Clair, "I think your wife is going to be all right, but I'm not sure about the baby." After the baby was born, I asked, "Is it a boy or girl?" The doctor said, "it is a girl, but she did not live." The full force of what happened did not hit me until later when the nurses brought babies to the other mothers...but not to me. Some friends sent me a magnificent azalea plant...and one afternoon as I lay looking at that beautiful plant with the afternoon sun streaming onto it, I was overwhelmed by a sense of peace and such a feeling that God was present with me. I could see His tracks...

By Appointment

 think one of the richest experiences I have had was in LaGrange, Georgia. The church was having a day of prayer and different people agreed to sign up for a segment of prayer time. Clair was out of town and I agreed to go at 3:00 on Saturday afternoon. As I drove the nine miles to the church, I was looking forward to the experience, but did not think too much about it. I parked in the parking lot, and started walking to the church. Even before I entered the church, I could feel God's presence. I was alone in the church – alone with God. It was an overwhelming experience – to have an appointment with the God of the Universe. I'm not sure how much I prayed words, but I could not stop weeping. Too many times we make appointments with other people. If we had an appointment with the President of the United States, we should not let anything sidetrack us. There are those times when we must make an appointment with God...and keep it. Again...He showed me His tracks, when I obeyed His wants.

Trinidad-Speech

nother time in Trinidad, I was preparing to speak to an interdenominational Christian Education meeting for ten minutes on Saturday morning. On Friday, new missionaries came from the States and when I went to bed at 1:00 AM I really did not know what I was going to say. As I lay there praying about it desperately, a whole outline came to me. ...and I thought it sounded pretty good. I definitely do not recommend waiting this late to prepare a talk, but God understands our circumstances and if we allow Him, He will always meet us where we are... And when we let Him work in these instances, His tracks become evident.

Decisions

hen we make decisions, God gives us an opportunity to see His tracks. Some decisions are major, some seem insignificant, but no matter how we rate the importance of the decision, it is important to allow God to lead us in that task.

For example, when Clair retired from the Board – but not from the Lord – we were approached to go to North Carolina as interim pastors. I was reluctant because there is always so much to arrange when you are going to leave your home for a while. One morning, before I got out of bed, (a good time for prayer), I realized I needed to pray about it and I told the Lord, "I don't want to move." Do you know what answer came back? "I moved!" As I thought about that, I realized if God could move all the way from heaven to earth to bring the knowledge of His love, I could surely at least move from Anderson to North Carolina.

God Talks with Me

 t was May of 1988. Clair and I were planning to go to the church, eat breakfast there, and help with workday. As I started getting cleaned up. My arm felt funny, sort of tingly, but it didn't stop there. My leg started to feel the same way. My hand began to draw up and then my leg. By this time I knew I was in trouble and so I called loudly, "Clair, come quickly." He came running and helped me sit down, then called the doctor who said to go to the emergency room. Clair called the ambulance—all during this time my body was drawing up more.

"Oh, Lord, am I going to be paralyzed? What is going to happen to me? There are things I still have to do! Will I be able to talk, walk, or write? Oh, Lord, help!"

It would be an hour before I could go for a cat scan and during that time many thoughts were going through my mind. If I am paralyzed I won't be able to do some of the things only I could do—such as co-author a book with my husband, finish some other writing I have in mind— things that are in my mind and that I need my body to accomplish. I must rearrange my priorities. Someone else can clean my house and take care of some other things, but no one else can know the way God helped us during all those years on the mission field and at home the ways He has shown us His tracks.

The tests came back okay; I could go home. The doctor decided I had a TIA—a transitory ischemic attack. What a stressful three hours, but it may have changed my life. During church the next morning I said to the Lord, "Here is my body, Lord. It's yours. Show me how to take care of it so I can accomplish the most for you."

As a result of this episode my doctor sent me to a neurologist, who sent me to a neurosurgeon, who sent me to another neurologist who took many, many tests. When it was all over, the doctor said I probably had primary lateral sclerosis, a deterioration of the spinal cord. This would not kill me. I would probably die from something else. But there was no cure for the sclerosis. I could find it harder and harder to walk and might have to use a wheelchair.

I did NOT have cancer, Aids, or a host of other terrible diseases for which I praised the Lord.

Since that time the Lord has spoken to me. The fact that I may not be able to walk is not the end of the world. A great many people have made tremendous contributions to society and have done great things from a wheelchair–like Franklin D. Roosevelt, who was elected four times as President of the United States. It may be that God will give me a different ministry than I have had in the past. I have a new understanding of the difference in values between the physical and the spiritual. No matter what happens to the body, I need not be affected. I am in existence for eternity.

Just as the shuttle, Challenger, loses the rocket pack and goes on and on, just so, the body that houses my spirit may fall off but I will go on forever. I can use whatever comes to me to God's glory. When I left the doctor's office he told me that if it became harder to walk, I should come see him and he would give me another MRI to see if there might be a surgery that would help. Am I worse? Do I need to go to the doctor?

One night as I was getting warm in bed I was asking the Lord if I should go to the doctor. It seemed he said to me, "No, I will take care of you." Just at that moment the song "God Will Take Care of You" began playing on the tape recorder. What an assurance! The God who made the universe, who filled the midnight sky with a billion stars, who engineered my body, said He would care for me! "Mighty God who holds the vast reaches of the universe, thank you for holding my frail life in your mighty hands!" *The tracks of God!*

Decisions~Kenya

Psalm 139

hen we were getting ready to go to Kenya on a one-year assignment, I was praying before I got out of bed in the morning. We were having to make many major arrangements in preparation to go, as we would be gone for an entire year. I was getting very tired and feeling low, so I asked the Lord, "Why are we going to Kenya anyway?" The answer came... "Because I want you there!"

And scriptures are full of tracks: Psalm 139:9-10 NIV

"If I rise on the wings of the dawn, (we were flying early in the morning to Kenya) if I settle on the far side of the sea, (Kenya is the other side of the world) even there your hand will guide me, your right hand will hold me fast." Talk about a TRACK !

Opportunities to Make Tracks!

od gives us opportunities to make tracks in our daily lives. Charles Allen, pastor of the Grace Methodist Church in Atlanta, tells how he "catches moments with God." On his way to the church he has to pass four "slow" stop lights. Instead of grumbling about them, he has worked out a devotional schedule for the lights.

1st LIGHT: "What am I most thankful for today?"

2nd LIGHT: "What have I done in the past 24 hours for which I am ashamed?" He confesses and asks God's forgiveness.

3rd LIGHT: "What is God's will for my life this one day?"

4th LIGHT: "Whom should I pray for today?"

In some sense, using these small opportunities, he was opening time and space for God to show His tracks.

Coincidence

Pat McCune

I recently experienced God's workings and almost missed the tracks!

My husband and I were dining out one evening and decided to drive by a business in town which had recently burned. As we passed the site, he pulled into an alley to get a better view.

Later that afternoon I drove to visit my parents and brother who live two hours from my home. It was dark before I arrived and I was alone, but the trip was seemingly uneventful. As I approached my parents' driveway I suddenly struck a very deep pothole and when I stopped the car..., in their drive..., the tire was completely flattened. I was irritated and voiced it. My brother assured me that the tire was replaceable and I was safe, but I was just upset.

The next morning my brother came into the house after checking the tire in the daylight and he asked me if I had noticed my steering pulling to the right on my drive to the house. I realized that I had noticed a slight pull when I applied the brakes at a stoplight in the town prior to my parents' hometown. My brother said he removed the flattened tire and a large screw was embedded in it. He said the tire was most likely losing air the whole time I was traveling and the pothole just finished the job.

I was suddenly struck by the "coincidence." God managed events so that I was with family and with able-bodied men who could help me when the tire flattened. And he prevented me from getting back on the road for the trip home without first addressing the problem.

This is a coincidence to some...but to me...it is God's tracks. He loves me and protects me, even when I don't deserve it.

Facial Expression-
Can Show Tracks of God

any years ago I was involved in a special revival service in a church in Minnesota. During the final night's service, the featured speaker was a doctor whose mother had donated a rather large amount of money from her estate to the Gideons. The money was to be used to place Bibles in places where many could have access to the Word.

The doctor was well known in the community and had been invited to offer a response concerning the gift he delivered on behalf of his deceased mother. As he thanked the church for their faithfulness in forwarding the money for its designated purpose, he began speaking of his own personal spiritual journeys and beliefs.

During his recitation, he told a beautiful story of an old man whom he had been treating for cancer. He related the heartfelt details of how the man's condition worsened in spite of medical intervention. He said the old man came to him for another examination and continued treatment. Upon seeing him, the doctor knew that the poor man's condition was deteriorating rapidly. After the examination, the doctor knew he must deliver the inevitable report that the old man was approaching the end of his days on this earth…death was near. The doctor prepared himself to deliver the bad news, but much to his surprise, as he shared the dire news, a broad smile lit up the old man's face, and he began thanking the doctor for the news! The doctor said the old man had the happiest, most joy-filled expression he had ever seen on a human face! The old man said he was happy to learn that he would be changing the course of his living…and would be moving to heaven.

As the doctor closed his recitation, he said to the congregation, "Friends, if I never see God for myself….I can say to you that I saw Him in the face of the old man that day when I told him he was soon to die!"

The Tracks of God -
An Unsolicited
Mind Boggling Letter

Unknown Author

It was just a few steps across the alley from my back door to the front door of the big, red-brick building next door, Central Avenue School in Anderson, Indiana. Just a small distance, but a giant leap — not for mankind, but for the skinny, awkward, self-conscious five-year-old that was me.

Mom and Dad never read the how-to parenting books of today and, even if such literature had been available, they wouldn't have been interested. Both were so preoccupied with their own lives and marital problems which finally led to their divorce, they spent little time interacting with my brother and me. Both were intelligent, but not the least interested in intellectual, cultural, or spiritual pursuits. I largely shifted for myself.

As we now know, children who are not read to and conversed with at a young age are often developmentally deprived and school can be difficult for them. What a fortunate child I was to attend an old-fashioned neighborhood school. No widely diversified curriculum, gymnasium, cafeteria or many of the other great facilities of modem education, just teachers who devoted their lives to the profession and loved kids. They taught in a system which allowed them to know each student and their home situations. And I knew them because they visited with me as a pre-schooler as I perched on our bank watching the kids on the playground. The teachers were my special friends.

I'm 72 years old now, but I can name each of them from kindergarten through junior high school. Just a few quick examples of why they mean so much to me. When I nearly died in second grade, Mrs. Capehart brought me the books of stories I loved to hear her read and lessons I could do at home. Later she bought copies of the same books for my grandchildren. Ms. Bronnenberg took me to her home for a weekend visit and had a tea party under the big tree in her front yard for me and the neighborhood kids. Mr. White called me "Susan Bamboosan, the gal of my choosin'" and took me to civic music concerts with his wife. They thought, or acted as if, I could do great things and because of that I set out to prove them right. They encouraged me to enter essay contests, speak at special events, tackle hard projects, be a leader. When I was well groomed, they told me I looked neat and pretty, after which I made every effort to be that way. Lack of attention at home caused me to be a people-pleaser, in this case a teacher-pleaser. Not always a good thing, but in this case a great thing.

These strong role models instilled in me a strong desire to follow in their footsteps as a teacher. Dwight and I married young and circumstances prevented my attending college then. But, when my kids were in second and fifth grade, I followed my dream in spite of being a busy pastor's wife and mother. What a blessing it was to me when I received that diploma. I've always battled an inferiority complex and that accomplishment helped me to cope when we later pastored a church attended by more than fifty educators.

When the odor of burning leaves permeate the fall air, I feel happy. It's my favorite season, probably because it reminds me of the start of a new school year which I always eagerly anticipated. When I pass that old school today, memories well up. I smell the smells and remember the faces and the joy I experienced there. Entering that door changed me forever.

The Tracks of God in Our Christian Journey

Gene W. Newberry

My friend, Clair Shultz, asked me if I would share my testimony about the Tracks of God in my Christian journey. The theme resonated quickly with me for that is really what I have been doing in my vocation for over seven decades—Tracking God, for myself and for others. Philip Yancey makes a bolder statement of it in his new book *Haggling with God*. There is a caution here—just so Yancey and we don't appear arrogant in our quest and tracking. There will be surprises along the way.

Isn't it fair to ask that we be humble and open as we follow the Tracks of God? We have eyes to see and ears to hear, and we'll keep them open. There is a lot of mystery in our question. God's ways and thoughts are higher than ours. But, the miracle and surprise are that God is also tracking us. Rev. 3:20 says, "Here I am! I stand at the door and knock. If anyone hears my voice and opens the door, I will come in...." I am talking with a couple of avowed atheists in the retirement village where we live. Our visits are friendly, but they have given up tracking. They are angry at the church and feel that God is a fantasy. I assure them that with our eyes of faith and our seeking hearts open, we will be surprised by the joy and discovery.

There are many, but I am going to suggest four of the Tracks of God that have meant most to me. First is the Word of God, the Bible. I memorized John 3:16 and the 23rd Psalm when I was a boy, and I often recite them at night before going to sleep. The Bible is God's self disclosing about himself, about life, about our destiny. In a sentence the Old Testament is the account of a nation, the Hebrew people, in their quest, mountains and valleys, toward monotheism, the truth of one God. The New Testament tells the beautiful story of their coming King, The Messiah, the Lord Jesus Christ and His love and will for all mankind.

The Bible is full of stories of God leaving His tracks for persons to observe, interpret, and follow. Read Matthew 13 for some beautiful examples. The Bible was centuries in the making, with these wonderful stories told and retold, before being written down. It is not a book of magical yarns. But, it tells the story of inspired people in their experiences, visions, and lessons in their travels toward and with God. Words like exodus and exile leap out at you and finally going home to live in the father's house. Through Hebrew, Latin, and Greek, the stories, the ancient word came down to us and finally landed in King James English in 1611.

You know we are going to say that God left His most obvious tracks in creation. There are purpose, order, beauty, and a good deal of mystery all around us. I visited my audiologist this week to be tested for hearing aids. On his wall he had a picture of the inner ear. I stood there amazed at the organ, the intricacy of the mechanism that makes my hearing possible. Is anyone going to tell me that the necessary body organs and their life-giving functions occurred just incidentally and accidentally? This is the design argument for God's hand and wisdom in creation. Almighty God is the purposeful Designer. Is evolution taking place? Of course, for God has been at work in His world for millions of years. I have no problem with this; it is even more miraculous for me and shows the marvelous Tracks of God in creation.

God is love as the scriptures say, and He shows it by sending His son, Christ, as our Redeemer. Yes, we trace the tracks directly to you and me. We know ourselves to be sinners, fallen and in need of divine forgiveness. Sometimes it is a frightfully dark picture; at others it is a modest turning around to hear the welcoming "Yes." God sent His son, Jesus Christ, to live among us and to die for us. And, Jesus gave us the guidelines, made the tracks, for us to follow to the father's house. Our souls have the emptiness just the right size for the love and forgiveness of God to fill. And, then He walks beside us all the way home. "Amazing Grace, how sweet the sound!"

Finally, let me sing the praises of the church. There are over two billion Christians on the earth, and I rejoice in saying that, for almost eight decades, I have been one of them. And, I am as embarrassed as anyone when a pastor or congregations on earth or on TV mishandle the Word or engage in some illegal activity. For shame, they sometimes happen. At their best the churches, next to our families, are the most beautiful islands of service and love on earth and display the Tracks of God to our eternal destiny. The church may have her critics but no real competitors.

The Tracks of God are wide and deep if we have eyes to see. Think with me of the story the Bible tells, the beauty and grandeur of God's creation, feeling the love of Christ shed abroad in our hearts, and finding the peace and power of God as we worship and serve in His church.

God Showed His Tracks
Bemidji, MN—Gas Money

We were there to start a new congregation of the Church of God. We did not have a regular salary. It was necessary to move in order to match our meager money flow. We finally were able to secure a very old, unused, frame church building in which to hold services and we moved into the basement of the building to live. It was half in the ground and half above the ground, with three-foot windows. This helped us save on our heating. Our cooking stove was a small two-burner propane gas plate which received fuel from a small tank outside the building. When we moved to this downstairs location we had to ask the gas company to move the tank for us. While it was being moved, the man from the gas company said, "Sir, you will have to replace this tank fairly soon for it is almost empty." I asked, "How do you know that?" He replied, "It goes by weight and it is very light to carry."

In those days a tank of propane gas cost $8.00 and with our budget we didn't see how we could get enough extra money to buy a new tank. Several months went by and there was still gas for the stove. Summer came and we drove to Anderson to visit our parents and attend the International Convention. We left a woman at the house to care for things and she used the gas plate until we got back. It was now the last of June and warm outside.

We decided to take a walk to Lake Bemidji to eat our lunch. Retha was cooking some potatoes to make potato salad when I heard the postman rattling our post box and I went upstairs to see what was there. I found one letter and brought it downstairs, looking to see who it was from. At that moment Retha asked me to turn the gas off since the potatoes were cooked. When I went to the stove I found the fire was out. I thought the wind had blown the flame out so I lit a match and threw it on the burner but nothing happened.

Then it dawned on me that the gas tank was empty and we still did not have money to pay for a new tank. Now what? I opened the letter and found a check for $10.00 with a note saying the donors had felt led of God to send the check. The money arrived at the same time our gas went out, but it had been mailed long before. *Tracks of God!*

God's Challenges

The effects of World War II were drawing America to become involved. In 1939, Europe was in grave difficulty. Germany had overrun many countries and these people were in great trouble. This situation was brought closer to home by one of the couples who had agreed to give some support to our new congregation. In one evening service with just a few people (seven or eight) in attendance, this man came in and sat behind me on the second bench. He leaned forward to say something and in a whisper he told me he would not be able to support me any longer. His family was suffering in Norway and he would have to use his tithe to help them. Then he said, "I will not be back again, and I suggest that it might be better if you go back to Anderson." He had been giving $25 a month. This was his agreement with the state ministers. So now our problems were increasing but that was not the end.

Sometime later we had gone about twenty-five miles through the snow to a place called Black Duck to hold an afternoon meeting in a home. These people were really isolated from any church and had asked me to come. After a bit of fellowship we had a worship service. To help with my driving expense they took an offering which totaled about eighty-seven cents. They thanked me and then we drove the twenty-five miles back to Bemidji. When we got back home and opened our mail we found a letter from one of the other three families. He was very critical of my sermons saying they were not biblical, that I was a heretic. In his four-page letter he called reference to point after point that I had made—he said I was completely wrong. His support was $10 a month which we used for rent. Because I had a wife and baby he would send his money through May, but then it would end. He added that he thought I should return to Anderson where I had come from.

The words of my brother came back to me—the words he spoke to me before I left Anderson. My brother's idea was to quit the ministry. My idea was to continue to give God the opportunity to turn things around. I remembered a time in the life of Jesus when everything went wrong—all forsook him, even his disciples, and he ended up on a cross. Yet that very rejection brought salvation to the world. Our seeming defeats often are what lead to some special victory. *Tracks of God!*

A Track in the Cold

Since we did not have a large congregation, we had time to answer a few calls for help from neighboring congregations in Minnesota and North Dakota. We had been asked by our pastor in Grand Forks, North Dakota, to hold a week of special services in the church and to speak on the radio broadcast every morning. We left Bemidji one morning very early, to drive to Grand Forks, about one hundred and twenty miles away. The temperature was five below zero and even with the car heater going full blast we could feel the cold coming through our heavy coats. The road was good though snow covered, and for many miles we never saw another car or house of any kind. We had driven several hours and all went well. It was near daylight when suddenly the motor began to miss and finally stopped. We coasted around a corner and as we came to a stop we saw we were right in front of a gas station. The man was opening the pumps and had heat. He was a mechanic and repaired our car while we were snug and warm inside the station. We heard the radio broadcast from Grand Forks when the announcer said he did not know where their special guests were. The "special guests" were listening to the broadcast about forty miles away.

In this frigid, sparsely settled area, why did the car stop right where we could stay warm and still have our car repaired? Jesus said, "Lo, I am with you always." – a track of God's care.

Tracks on the Mission Field

That Happened Among Us.

n this article I have been trying to write about the God who is unseen, but can be recognized and partly seen by the tracks of experiences and activities we see. What kind of tracks? Tracks like those left on our earth, which I have already mentioned. Some of these situations where tracks are seen – like the footprint of a rabbit, the footprint of a lion. To recognize a lion, one only has to see a track that is left in the dirt. Often times things happen without seeing the source or how it was done. For example, electricity is not visible but one can know what it is if he touches a wire that is charged with electricity. One can send a message 5,000 miles and never see the recipient.

One illustration of God's tracks: When we were in Trinidad, West Indies, we were trying to find a house in which we could place our students when they came to The West Indies Bible Institute. The students were coming and we had no place to put them. However, when it was almost time to begin the Bible school, a young girl came to our door, rang the doorbell and asked us if we knew of anyone who wanted to rent a house. Yes, we certainly did need a place to put our students. How come we were asked by an absolute

Retha teaching in Tobago

*Left to Right: Cliff Barrows, Billy Graham, Joe Blinco, Horace Fenton, Clair Shultz
(Clair was Chairman of the Billy Graham Crusade in Trinidad)*

stranger about a house, when we didn't even have a sign of advertising about our great need? We did not even have a sign in the yard. And the house was between our house and the Port-of-Spain church – both places where classes were taught.

One of the things we wanted to do when we got to Trinidad, West Indies, was to see how the church work was going which had previously been started before we arrived on the scene. We noted one small church, which had never grown much, located about fifty miles from Port of Spain, the main city of the Island. It had possibly fifteen people who identified themselves with its membership. The church looked more like a small rundown barn – old, unpainted wood, open spaces where formerly windows used to protect the inside from the weather. One had to be careful when walking he did not get his foot in a hole in the wood floor. After an inspection we decided that the two of us – two missionaries – would have to make the place look like a live church.

So we worked on the floor first and made other repairs to make the building safer. We had a few solid benches and we had one pressure gas lamp which hung directly over the podium. When I would speak the light gathered many kinds of insects.

After preaching a couple of sermons, at the close of the meeting, a woman came forward to pray and I knelt to talk to her. She was living with a man who was not legally her husband and she had seven or eight children. I then met her the next day to explain what was needed if she were to become a real Christian.

She wanted to become a Christian, but if she did she should marry her live-in "husband" or leave the living situation. She came to church every night but her mate stayed outside and looked through an open window. The windows were all open and one could get the teaching about marriage and church without even entering the building. He could hear the message through the open windows.

This may seem like a difficult situation to deal with but it is not for the Lord. Things happened and in time both of them became interested in the will of God.

Both of them attended an afternoon meeting in their region and asked me about marriage. In time both were following the Lord in their best knowledge. And both were silently following the Lord as they were able. After this incident, several months passed by and we were making plans to return to the States for our furlough. But that was not the end. Several hours before we left, I heard someone rattling our yard gate. I ran down to greet this couple then. Of all things, they wanted to get married before I left for our furlough. They already had their marriage license and were ready to be married then. We were scheduled to fly home about 1 p.m. So, at that time, we walked to the church, about a block away, and I married them. We then left for the States for our furlough.

After a six-month furlough we returned to Trinidad again. The marriage worked for both of them. One of their oldest sons had become a pilot to fly one of the large planes back and forth to the United States.

The Witch Woman
— Grenada

nother time Ralph Coolidge and I visited Grenada. This time we stopped at a place several miles from the airport called Marqui Village, situated several hundred feet from the ocean. An East Indian man was the laypastor of this work. He had a small sailboat that he used to catch fish for a living. Eight or ten people comprised his flock. It was an area where many nutmeg, clove and cinnamon trees were grown.

We soon learned about a very grave problem they were having. The small building where they had their worship service was located about a stone's throw from the ocean; however, a witch-like woman who lived in the area began to claim that the land where this church building was placed belonged to her. Why she believed as she did I do not know since the building had been in that location for many years. She made it her concern to try to destroy the building and the benches in it. She broke into the building by tearing off the lock and jabbing the walls many times with her panga (big knife), breaking all the windows. They repaired the openings with pieces of tin and then she would even punch holes through the tin. They were afraid of her, thinking she might come and burn down their houses at night.

When we heard these stories, we began to become a little fearful ourselves. The local people provided housing for us. A sister who owned a very small house, about eight by twelve feet, moved out and turned her home over to us to use while we were there. The bedroom was so small the bed was touching three walls, leaving a space of about three feet on one side so that one could get into the bed. The house did not have windows but rather small doors that were opened during the day and closed at night.

Now when you are the only two white people in the community, everyone knows of your arrival. The witch woman knew it too. We wondered whether the window-doors, about waist high from the ground, should be left open or closed when we went to bed. The problem was that the heat of the day made everywhere in the little house hot. Getting ready for bed and feeling the heat, we decided that we would have to leave at least one window open, the one that was three feet away, on the side where one entered the bed. There were no electric lights around. All we had was a kerosene lamp and a flashlight. We looked at the open window and it scared us. All this woman would have to do was to pass by and throw a lighted torch onto our bed which was covered with a mosquito net. We would have been caught in a blaze of fire immediately. What to do?

We decided to make a booby trap at the open window that would waken us if she approached. We placed a folding, canvas-covered deck chair on its end, on a small stand in front of the open window-door. That blocked most of the opening and the canvas could flop in the breeze. Then we took a metal basin used for washing one's hands, stood it on edge and placed the lip just under the bottom of the chair leg to hold it in that upright position. The slightest movement would allow it to fall to the floor. If the woman touched the chair to slide it away, the basin would fall with a bang. We put out our kerosene lamp, crawled under the mosquito net and stretched out to sleep. A full moon was shining brightly so we had a little vision outside the window. A large banana leaf would occasionally swing out over the window giving an image that might look like a person's shadow in front of the opening, but in a little while both of us dozed off to sleep.

Suddenly I was awakened by the voice of Coolidge yelling loudly, "You get out of here." I raised up with flashlight in hand looking around the room. I looked at the window and the canvas on the chair was still flopping in the breeze and the basin was still standing on its edge, held down by the chair leg. I whispered to Ralph, "Where is she? Where is she?" I could hardly move because when I raised up so quickly my head got caught in the mosquito net, yanking it down tight around me. I was not only scared but also bound. In a moment, Coolidge fell back on his pillow and said, "Oh, I must have been dreaming. I thought I was lying here on the bed looking at the sky, when through the window the witch woman came with a big panga (knife) in her hand, ready to use it on me." Learning he had a nightmare, we both relaxed a bit, but then decided to remove the chair and close and lock the window opening. We then dozed off and got a little more sleep.

At dawn's light, we were awakened by voices outside the house and several people passing up and down the road. I dressed a bit and opened the door to ask some of the men the cause of all the excitement. They explained that the witch woman had gone to the church, broken open the door, broken some of the benches into pieces, also the pulpit, and burned them as firewood. Even though she had been causing trouble that night, we still decided to go ahead with our plans to have a service at ten o'clock that morning. We went down to the building where some folks were gathering for the worship. Some were carrying chairs to sit on. We began the service and I led the singing and the worship exercises. Coolidge had just started to preach when all of a sudden I saw every head turn, looking out the windows. I looked, too, and saw the witch woman coming around the corner of the building. She looked very dirty and ill clad, carrying a basket in one hand and a large panga in the other. She slowly walked in and came directly towards us in front. Finally, she stopped, looked on the right side, reached and grabbed the hands of the woman who owned the house where we were staying. She yanked on her arms saying, "You come out of here. You come out of here. You come out of here." The house owner finally jumped up and began to push her. Soon they were shoving each other up and down the aisle. All the while, Coolidge was preaching, but he had lost his audience. Finally a large, young man, sitting next to the aisle, maybe twenty years old, jumped up, grabbed her by the arm, twisted it, and said, "You come out of here," and pushed her outside. She finally disappeared, cursing as she went. We had to dismiss the meeting. God's protection – *Track of God.*

After that we walked about a mile to see the magistrate of the area. We told him about the problem and asked if there wasn't something that could be done to stop this woman from her deviltry. Answer: "Yes, we can have her put in jail, if the church will pay for her keep while she is in jail." That was a new way of thinking for us, hard to manage! The point was that nothing could be done. Only God could handle it. When one reads the New Testament, the story of the early church, one could imagine he was almost going back to those days. The devil is still working overtime to destroy the church. What was the solution to the problem in Grenada? Well, in time we did get some graduate students able to go there, live and work full-time in the church.

Family Life in a Strange Culture

I n a foreign community like Trinidad, our children faced many problems as they grew up. When they were both small, their care was much like that of any other country. They needed parental loving care and we did try to give them just that playing games with them, helping them with their juvenile problems, reading stories to them at night and rubbing their backs when they went to bed. We did establish one rule that held most of the time. We would take Friday off from our mission work. Every Friday afternoon we would go to a beautiful ocean beach. It was up and over a range of mountains, just fourteen miles from home. It was good to play and splash in the warm water, hunt for shells, watch the giant waves break and roll to the shore as we rode ahead of them on surf boards. Near the close of the day, on the way home we would stop at a wide place, high over the ocean below, and cook our supper using a charcoal pot. In silence, we would often watch the sun go down over the ocean and sometimes watch the moon come up. We watched the *tracks of God*.

Tracks in Africa

The scripture affirms that not anyone has seen God but we can see His tracks which He leaves in His work. What I want to do is to show you how God has worked in places like Africa. We spent nine years working there and learned much about what had been done and what was still being done. I would like to tell you how the tracks of God were left there by one of our first converts, a man named John Owenga. He was there just a couple of years before we got there and here is his story.

When the missionaries first went to Africa, one of the Africans who listened to their story was John Owenga, a rank pagan. He stood near the missionaries as they told about Jesus, who He was and what He did and how He was still wanting to find people who would accept His teaching and explain it to others.

When he heard the missionaries tell the full story of Jesus coming to this world and what He came to do, he was deeply touched and wanted to go immediately to tell his people about Jesus. In time, he gathered two other men and walked across miles of rough timber land and tall grass to the country of Uganda, telling the story of Jesus, who He was, and what He came to do. They ate what they could find along the way with offerings the people gave them. They had covered much of the country telling the people the story when he got sick and could go no farther. Some of the people tried to help him but, in spite of their help, he died on the way. Now, far from home, what would the other two who were with him do with his body? They tried to find a place to bury his body

but no one would give them a place to bury him. So they had to burn his body. Then they went back to Kenya and told the story. In person, I heard this story as it was told to several thousand people.

In Kenya there is a marker in front of the Kima Cathedral, bearing his name which reads "In memory of John Owenga who gave his life to tell his neighbors in Uganda about Jesus." John was one of the first converts in Kenya, who laid down his life for the people of the world. *THE TRACKS OF GOD!*

Contrary Winds

ll of us have had narrow escapes, difficulties that could have brought an end to our life on earth. Several senior missionaries, along with myself, attended an interdenominational leadership conference in the highlands of Kenya, 7,000 feet altitude. Our group had lodging in a little cottage to ourselves with bunk beds. Because of the high altitude and cold climate, each cottage had a wood-burning fireplace to heat the room. We didn't see any wood, so we looked around and found several old branches which we broke up and with some old paper started a fire. It started to burn and, because it was time for the service, we locked the door and went to the first conference. On returning to our room, we opened the door and found the room full of smoke. Apparently, birds had built a nest in the stack so the fire did not get proper draft to burn. On seeing all the smoke, we opened the door wide and some windows and took some towels to fan out the smoke. We worked to get the room clear but with the fresh air, we also fanned in a lot of cold, damp air. We felt we did not dare go to sleep without fresh air in the room no matter the cold air. My bunk was right under a slightly open window. By morning, I came down with a fever, which got worse as the morning progressed. By noon we decided we must drive the two hundred miles back to Kima, our residence. Now what?

At home, my condition worsened and by the second day we decided we had to go to our mission hospital, twenty miles away. On the way to the hospital over dusty, bumpy roads Clair said, "If I die, take my body back home. I don't want to be buried here." Our own doctor was gone on a medical trip to Uganda, so a doctor from the Friends Mission had agreed to serve our hospital during his absence. When we reached the hospital a gurney was waiting for me and I was taken to X-ray my lungs. After reading the X-ray the doctor said, "Pastor Shultz, the news is not good. You have viral pneumonia. You will have a long, difficult recovery, maybe six months." The next day our own young doctor, William Anderson, returned and took over my care; however, after a week I was not making any progress.

The Mission Hospital could not give the ultimate care I needed. The doctor wanted to give the best care possible, so he took me and my hospital bed to a private bedroom in his own home where he could give the best attention to my needs day or night. As for a doctor's help, I have never had it so good. His wife, Bea, tended to my needs and helped with my care.

I was so weak I could hardly eat or do anything for myself. One day I could hardly breathe and called for oxygen. Retha was very worried and wondered what would happen to her if I should die. She was so upset the nerves in her shoulder felt twisted into a knot. One day I asked her to read Mark 6:45-51. This scripture tells of the disciples who had just been through the thrilling experience of seeing Jesus feed 5,000 people with only five loaves and two fishes. Jesus had told them to get into the boat and go to the other side and he would come later. He went into the nearby mountain to pray. During the night a storm came up and they could hardly handle the boat *for the wind was against them* (as the wind was against us). They looked up and saw something white coming toward them. They were thoroughly frightened for they thought they saw a ghost. They screamed but Jesus said, "*Be not afraid. It is I.*" Then He got into the boat with them and the wind ceased!

As we read this story we realized that we were in a similar situation. We were having a storm and could hardly navigate. As we meditated on the fact that Jesus saw them and came to them in their trouble, it seemed we could see Jesus, Clair, and Retha in a little boat riding up and down the tempestuous waves, but we had the assurance that so long as Jesus was in the boat the storm would end and all would be well. A great peace came over us and we were able to let go and let God get on with the healing process—which He did in His own time.

My recovery was very slow. I was so weak I could scarcely take one step. I would try to walk two steps from one chair to another, sit down and rest awhile and then move the distance of two chairs again. In truth, it was about six months before I was able to pick up the pressures of my work again. Dr. Anderson is still my physician here in the States since both of us have returned from our missionary work abroad. What memories we have as we are still together.

On the Brink of Disaster

In 1976, I led a group of fifteen on a "Venture in Missions" tour to East Africa, visiting our mission stations to see just how missions worked. After our tour ended, I escorted the group to the airport in Nairobi, where they would board a plane and return to the States. As a Mission Board representative overseeing East Africa, I had to go to Tanzania for about a week to deal with a problem which desperately needed my help. With that finished, I was ready to board my plane and head back to the States myself. However, upon arriving at the airport at Moshi, Tanzania, I learned that my flight had been canceled. What was I supposed to do?

One of the missionaries suggested that his son, Gary, take one of their cars and drive me to Nairobi and I could still catch my scheduled flight. I thanked him for the idea and so we started by car toward Nairobi. We came to the Kenya border about 8:00 P.M., went through customs and immigration, purchased gasoline and again started on our way. The road was good, new blacktop, made by the Americans, and the moon was full, really bright. One could almost drive without headlights. No traffic. No cars. Because conditions were so good, I was not wearing a seat belt. My biggest mistake. It almost cost me my life. About 8:30 P.M., I looked at my watch and told the driver we would be in Nairobi almost the same time the plane would have arrived, had it flown. The next thing I realized was that my head was really wrapped tight with a cloth around it and I was lying on a small bed someplace. A young African nurse was putting IV fluids in my arm. I asked, "How did I get here?" She said, "Someone brought you here. You were in an automobile accident." I asked, "What time is it?" She replied, "1:30 A.M." I was in one of the small government clinics where members of the primitive Masaai tribes were treated.

In about a half hour I was conscious enough to talk to Gary, who told me what happened. As we traveled over a slight hill on the road, we came upon a large herd of goats. He tried to miss the herd, applied the brakes and the car skidded to the side of the road, hit an embankment and flipped over, end over end, three times. I was thrown through the windshield and they found me right beside one of the front wheels lying on the sand. The place where the accident happened was very isolated. The driver held onto the steering wheel and was not hurt badly so was able to crawl out of the wreckage. He went back to the road to see if he could get help. A car came from Tanzania with an East Indian official of the Kenyan government in it. He drove us to a clinic, about six miles from the accident.

They did not know it at the time, but I had fifteen broken ribs, a very bad head and scalp injury, a broken nose and a bad hip injury. Fortunately, a Dutch doctor had come to Kenya to this clinic that very day to help these primitive people. I was one of his unexpected patients. A doctor from Holland was my caretaker. He probably saved my life because he knew what to do in this emergency—gave me IV fluids because I had lost so much blood, and sewed up my head. I was conscious for only about a half hour and then was out of it again until the next morning. At that time, I was placed in the back of a Land Rover and taken about fifty miles to the Nairobi hospital.

Retha's turn: I was in Anderson getting ready for Clair's return from Nairobi when Board officers came and told me that Clair had been in an accident. I thought they were kidding but soon realized that it was the truth. I called Nairobi and decided I had to go to Clair. Juanita Leonard had just returned from a stint there, so Clyde and Rowena Harting took me to see her. She sat in the middle of her bed in Indianapolis, called Nairobi, and made arrangements for me to stay with a friend who lived near the hospital where Clair had been for a week. I landed in Nairobi at night, missionaries met me and took me to this friend. In the morning, I walked to the hospital to see Clair. He looked like a zombie with his head all bandaged and his eyes black and blue. We were so glad to see each other.

He stayed in the hospital another week and every day I walked to the hospital from this friend's house. When he was released from the hospital, we moved to an Anglican guest house where the workers remembered us from our work in Kenya. They gave Clair the best of care.

As soon as he was able to walk, the doctor released him and we headed for home. We landed in Brussels, Belgium, where an ambulance took us to our hotel. The next day we flew to New York, which took nine hours instead of eight because of head winds. When we were landing in New York the pilot suddenly zoomed up again. We had almost missed the runway because of bad weather. After one night in a hotel, we flew to Indianapolis, but no one was there to meet us since the Board had not received our message. We called and they came for us. We were soon safely home, thanks to *tracks of God*. The accident happened on October 9, 1976 and Clair did not get to work again until March 5, 1977.

Miraculous Help in Kenya—Rift Valley

God does not necessarily have to work through people we know, or even people of faith. God worked through Pharaoh's daughter to save Moses. It is most interesting that the evil powers that took the Israelites to Babylon as slaves were the same powers God used to help them return to their homeland. The King even provided the money to rebuild their temple again (Ezra 1:1-4).

When I was working in Kenya I had some serious problems with stress. The problems of the work were so different than those at home and it was up to me to help direct our mission in its ongoing efforts. Usually we found medical help through local doctors; however, sometimes we thought we might get a better grasp of the problems we faced if we could talk to an American doctor. We found an American doctor working in a mission hospital located on the ridge of the Rift Valley. I made an appointment, saw the doctor, then went to a guest house to spend the night.

During the night a hard, lingering rain came down. Roads in the country are usually just dirt roads. When the roads are dry they are very dusty, and rain turns them into very slippery mud. The next morning we saw the road was bad, but thought we could go on, so we started. Soon we started up a slight incline and the car began to skid sideways and even turn around. When we had come to a complete stop we saw a man walking a short distance ahead of us, coming toward us. He came over and spoke to us saying there was no way we could drive on the road. He reminded us that there was another way that would take us to the highway, but it was a tricky road to follow, and we might get lost. He said, "If you want me to, I will get in the car with you and direct you so you can reach the highway. When we get there, I will walk back and finish my own journey."

He helped me turn the car around, traveled with us, told us to turn here and there, with no road signs to guide us and finally, with his help, we saw the paved road just ahead. When we stopped the car, he got out, said goodbye and started walking back to his former place on the road. Who was he? We had no idea. Did he ask for a tip or money? No! It was a bit strange that he happened to be right there when we were sliding off the road, even helped reverse the car, so it slid over where it should be, and then acted as our guide to the highway. *The Tracks of God!*

La Plume

In the study of language it helps one understand and learn an unfamiliar language if a photo or picture of that work is available. For example, the French word for "pen" is *la plume*. It is easier to remember the word if we see the word *la plume* associated with

I have a friend who wants his children to learn the Spanish language. He tried and tried to teach them the words, but to no avail. Finally, he hired someone who spoke the language as their native tongue. This lady began attaching signs to common, every day items, labeling them by their Spanish names. The children could then associate the words to something real...and so they learned!

And so it is much easier to know God because He gave us Jesus, who said, "he who has seen me has seen the Father," that we might see Him and understand His ways.

My Unchanging Walk with the Lord

by Clair Wilson Shultz

I've always been seeking a walk with the Lord
Where His presence is real, and I rest on His word.
But at times my busyness clutters my way
With things of the moment which soon pass away.

I keep telling myself, "I must make a change.
My schedule and life-style, I must rearrange."
The burden of guilt which cuts like a knife
Spurs me on to that walk with the Lord of all life.

Now is the time, while swift seasons roll,
to maximize time to develop my soul.
Before my demise and I'm under the sod,
I'd like to make sure that I'm walking with God.

When I start down life's mountain to that wide open plain
Where the trail disappears and no road-marks remain;
When the stars have all vanished and life's journey looks grim,
Then forever and ever, I'll be walking with Him.

The Ultimate Track of God

Jesus Christ!

he absolute and ultimate Track which shows the evidence of the existence of God is the gift of His Son, Jesus Christ. (John 1:18). No man has ever seen God, but God the only Son is very close to the Father. And the Son has shown us what God is like. Philip said to Jesus, "Lord show us the Father, and that is enough for us," to which Jesus replied… "he who has seen me has seen the Father." Jesus Himself was and is a Track of God.

To know and understand Jesus is to know and understand God. What do we learn about God from His Son?

- Jesus showed us that God, the Creator of the universe and all that exists, entered this world through an ordinary home and an ordinary family.

- Jesus showed us that God understands and identifies with the working man. He didn't just enter our world as a "King"…He existed as a working man…a carpenter.

- Jesus showed us that God understands temptation as He was tempted in many ways…just as we are every day. And through His life, we see that God understands "struggles." The life of Jesus was a life filled with struggles, not a life of serenity. But

Jesus

Jesus shows us that God can transform us through our struggles. We cannot be defeated if we travel through these struggles trusting in God to lead our way and be our strength and wisdom.

- Jesus showed us that God loved children. He traveled constantly, spreading the love of God to all who would listen...yet He made time to speak to the little children. "Let the little children come to me. Don't stop them, because the kingdom of heaven belongs to people who are like these children..." (Matthew 19:14).

- Jesus shows us a loving God. A God who cares intensely...so intensely that He offered His only Son as a sacrifice...to die for our sins. He allowed His Son to bear the wounds that we might be set free.

- Jesus showed us that God forgives sinners. (John 8: 3-11) "The teachers of the law and the Pharisees brought a woman there. She had been caught in adultery. They forced the woman to stand before the people."...and stated that the Law of Moses commanded them to stone the woman for her deed. They questioned Jesus what he thought about this. Jesus knew they were testing Him, so he knelt and drew on the ground...but they pressed him further. Jesus replied, "Is there anyone here who has never sinned? The person without sin can throw the first stone at this woman." And after hearing His words, they all left. Jesus then turned to the woman and said, "Woman, all of those people have gone. Has no one judged you guilty? ...So I also don't judge you. You may go now, but don't sin again." He didn't just free her from a painful death... He bid her to go and sin no more. But even more, He gave her the power to live above the sin.

- Jesus showed us that God heals people who are desperately ill. He healed the woman with the blood illness which had lasted for twelve years (Mark 5:25) "She had heard the reports about

Jesus and came up behind him in the crowd and touched his garment. For she said, 'If I touch even his garments, I shall be made well.' ...and she felt in her body that she was healed of her disease." And Jesus healed a man who was blind from birth. He even healed his good friend, Lazarus, and the little girl...after they had experienced death!

(Matthew 11:2-5) John the Baptist was in prison, but he heard about the things Christ was doing. So John sent some of his followers to Jesus. They asked Jesus, "Are you the man who John said was coming, or should we wait for another one?" Jesus answered, "Go back to John and tell him about the things you hear and see: The blind can see. The crippled can walk. People with harmful skin diseases are healed. The deaf can hear. The dead are raised to life. And the Good News is told to the poor."

Let us see what Henry Gariepy says about Christ in his book "100 Portraits of Christ."

"Many have tried to escape the force of this declaration. However Scripture, history and human experience corroborate its sacred and sublime truth.

In John's prologue to his Gospel, he gives us a breathtaking opening statement that declares the transcendent truths about Jesus Christ.

- He was eternally existent – "In the beginning was the '*Word*.'"
- He had fellowship with God – "and the Word was with God."
- He was God – "and the Word was God."

In that same prologue we read, "All things were made through him. Nothing was made without him." (John 1:3). The same truth is reaffirmed in the Pauline text of Colossians 1:16. Jesus is declared to have been an Agent of Creation. Before He ever came to earth, His hands tumbled solar systems and galaxies into space. He set the stars on their courses. He kindled the fires of the sun. He scooped out the giant beds of our mighty oceans.

This book deals with the subject of learning about God, as a real entity, present always and desiring to show Himself to every one of us if we will just take the time to see Him."

His holy fingers formed the bough
Where grew the thorns that crowned His brow,
The nails that pierced the hands were mined
In secret places He designed.

He made the forests whence there sprung
The tree on which His holy body hung,
He died upon a cross of wood
Yet made the hill upon which it stood.

The sun which hid from Him its face
By His decree was poised in space.
The sky which darkened o'er His head
By Him above the earth was spread.

The spear that spilt His precious blood
Was tempered in the fires of God.
The grave in which His form was laid
Was hewn in rocks His hands had made.

— F. W. Pitt

He created not only the macroscopic with its fiery planets and its unimaginable reaches of intergalactic space, but He created the microscopic as well. He polished the eye of every tiny insect, painted the bell of the lily, and crafted the exquisite geometry of the snowflake. He is the One who has made "all things bright and beautiful, all things great and small."

He is the Mighty God in His preincarnate glory and splendor. He was mighty in His birth when time was invaded by eternity and split in two. He was mighty in His ministry and His incomparable miracles. He was mighty in His teachings, putting the imperishable truths of the kingdom into word forms so indestructible that man could never forget them. He was mighty in His death as He rescued us from the hell we deserve and made us heirs to the heaven we forfeited. He was mighty in His resurrection as He arose, the Mighty Conqueror, over man's last enemy. He will be mighty as He comes again in His matchless and transcendent glory.

Mighty God, who holds the vast reaches of the universe, thank You for holding my frail life in Your mighty hands.

The writer of Hebrews sets forth Christ's credentials as God the Creator – "through whom He made the universe." He made the Sea of Galilee as well as hushed it. He could restore the blind man's sight, for He first made the optic nerve and retina. He could give hearing to the deaf man, for He first set the drum in the ear. He could cure the withered arm, for He made the bone and strung the muscle.

The Christ who walked the dusty roads of Galilee was the God who had roamed through the paths of galaxies. The Christ who lit the lakeside fire on which to cook breakfast for His tired, hungry disciples, had lit a billion stars and hung them across the midnight sky. He who asked the outcast for a drink had filled with water every river, lake, and ocean. Christ became God's self-disclosure. In Jesus, God entered humanity, eternity invaded time.

(Excerpts from "100 Portraits of Christ" by Henry Gariepy)

Love Letter

From Lafayette, GA newsletter

*D*ear...

I just had to write to tell you how much I love you and care for you. Yesterday, I saw you walking and laughing with your friends; I hoped that soon you'd want me to walk along with you, too. So, I painted you a sunset to close your day and whispered a cool breeze to refresh you. I waited – you never called – I just kept on loving you.

As I watched you fall asleep last night, I wanted so much to touch you. I spilled moonlight onto your face – trickling down your cheeks as so many tears have. You didn't even think of me; I wanted so much to comfort you.

The next day I exploded a brilliant sunrise into glorious morning for you. But you woke up late and rushed off to work – you didn't even notice. My sky became cloudy and my tears were the rain.

I love you. Oh, if you'd only listen. I really love you. I try to say it in the quiet of the green meadow and in the blue sky. The wind whispers my love throughout the treetops and spills it into the vibrant colors of all the flowers. I shout it to you in the thunder of the great waterfalls, and compose love songs for birds to sing for you. I warm you with the clothing of my sunshine and perfume the air with nature's sweet scent. My love for you is deeper than any ocean and greater than any need in your heart. If you'd only realize how I care.

My Dad sends His love. I want you to meet Him – He cares, too.

Fathers are just that way. So, please call on me soon. No matter how long it takes, I'll wait – because...

I LOVE YOU,

JESUS

If you have seen me... you have seen the father!